Can You Sell It?

A simple guide on how to be successful in both sales and relationships, because they're not so different.

John Yehl

Copyright © 2019 John Yehl

All rights reserved.

ISBN:
ISBN-13:978-1725049185

Dedication

To my wife and best friend, Becky. If she had any selling skills, I never would have written this book.

John Yehl

Foreword

STOP! You need to read this section. If you are like me, you probably skip over the forward because it is some mindless dribble that the author wrote to fill a few pages and tell you about his great accomplishments in life. I wish I could fill up a few pages with those kinds of accolades, but I don't have them and quite frankly I'm not sure I want them.

I do not have any formal training in the human psyche, nor am I a prize-winning economist with a PhD. I am not a trained counselor in marriage or relationships. I have never been a senior officer of a fortune five hundred company. I am just a guy who has been in sales for twenty-five years and been married about as long. I have worked my entire life to make a decent living.

I decided to write this book because of a discussion my wife and I had one night in bed. She asked me to perform a cleaning task for my in-laws, which I promptly refused. I knew that I would end up doing it, but for once, I wanted to have a little control. The next day I started writing this book.

This book is not intended to be the end-all cure-all for making it in business. Nor is it the bible for building a great salesperson or a great marriage. There are many great authors out there who are much smarter than me who can help you if you're looking for building blocks to a successful career or life. I have read a few, and some are pretty good. You may want to check them out... after you read my book.

This book takes a simple and humorous look at what it takes to become a successful sales person and have a happy marriage. I wanted this to be an easy read that both men and women could enjoy and maybe take something away from it. With my simple steps that apply to both sales and married life, you can live a lot longer and happier. This is not rocket science, and it's nothing new.

It's just something that we all forget once in a while. Hopefully my mix of humor and real-world encounters will help. If not, see a counselor, psychiatrist, priest, guru, motivational speaker, psychic, or Dr. Phil. Maybe they can help, but I cannot.

Chapter 1
Introduction

So, on one particular night I went to bed later than I should have. I stayed up watching television until eleven-thirty, knowing full well I had to get up at five o'clock the next morning to drive to see my dealer (At the time I was a factory sales rep for a fortune 100 company and our product is distributed through a dealer network). It was a bad idea I know, but I knew I had five and half good hours of sleep and the local gas station would have coffee made in the morning. What I didn't count on was my wife Becky wanting to ask me questions that night.

Let me preface this by telling you that I am a creature of habit. When I go to bed, I get ready, brush my teeth, watch a few minutes of television and fall asleep. My philosophy is that bed time is for sleep (and maybe one other thing), not a time for long conversations. I have informed Becky of this many times in the past, but for some reason, she always wants to start a conversation when we go to bed. This night was no different.

Becky came up after I was already in bed. As she was getting ready, she asked me if I would clean the iron deposits in her parent's shower. We live outside the city and right next door to her parents. We have well water with a high content of iron in the water which leaves an orange stain in the shower after some time. Her parents are getting older and it is getting harder for them to perform some household jobs, so we have been helping them. I have no idea how this subject evolved. We hadn't talked about this before and her parents have never brought up the subject. The only thing I can think of is that she saw the bottle of iron remover under the sink. I used it on our shower to remove the iron deposits from the well a few weeks earlier. I clearly did an amazing job, and it must have given her the idea.

It was a simple enough request, and asking me any other time than right before bed would have gotten the response of "Sure, I'll get to it as soon as I have time." That is normally code for it is not a pressing problem so I'll move it to the bottom of the priority list, but I will get it done. I think that was the response she thought she would get.

I, on the other hand, only had one idea on my mind at that time; it was how fast I could get to sleep. I really didn't think about what she was asking, I just said the first thing that I thought would end this conversation quickly. I said "no." Boy, was that the wrong answer! Don't get me wrong, I knew I was going to end up doing this if she wanted me to. I have been married long enough to know that I do not have a choice in the matter. It was part of the vows I stated when we got married; to obey. But this came out of left field, I never saw it coming. So, my mouth reacted before I had a chance to think.

What happened after that was a barrage of "whys" from my wife. The only answer I could give back was "because."

Normally I am a little more intelligent in my comebacks, but as I said earlier, it was late and I wanted to get to sleep. Then she tried to sell me on the idea with statements like, "You like to do things for my parents," and "You said it wasn't that hard when you did our shower." I was tired, and was watching the minutes click away on the clock by the bed. All I wanted was to get to sleep. She knew that. After a few minutes of conversation, I told her I wasn't going to do it because I did not want to. The clock was approaching midnight, and I had lost another potential half hour of sleep. Becky was exasperated with me, so I would not be getting to sleep any time soon.

I woke up the next morning a little tired, but the coffee at the gas station helped remedy that situation. Normally, I'm not a big dragger, nor do I rehash situations from the past, but I could not help myself regarding the previous night's conversation. So, on my long drive to the dealer's location, I began replaying the conversation from last night in my head. The thoughts soon began coming out of my mouth and I found myself talking to the steering wheel in my rental car. I can only imagine if someone was driving by and saw me. I'm sure it was quite a sight. Thankfully for me, it was still dark out. I kept thinking to myself, it wasn't fair the way she sprung the question on me. Plus, her timing was way off. Becky knows how I feel about bed time. I became a little upset with her. The longer I drove, the more I practiced my speech to her about how unfair it was to ask me that question at that time of the night. I was going to call her right then, but I was trying to be polite. I decided to wait a few hours, since I didn't want to wake her up too early. I realize now that it would have been a good lesson to teach her, but I also knew that sometimes it is better to think than act on some ideas. I decided that when we talked about it later, I would give her an analogy of how unprofessional this would have been if I would have used the same techniques in trying to sell a customer.

That's when it hit me; the inspiration for this book. She didn't mean to make me angry; she is a very intelligent person. She just did not have the proper selling skills to sell me on the idea. I started running through scenarios that she could have used to convince me to do this task for her parents. I was so excited I came up with a plan for her to convince me to clean her parents' shower (I'm not sure what they put in the coffee I bought that morning, but maybe I should have had a drug test the next day). I started relating it to some of the training I have done with my dealer sales people and the mistakes I have seen them make. That is when it happened.

I pulled over immediately, since it is not safe to drive and write. I started writing down the five ideas that every sales person and married person needs to know in order to be successful. I became very proud of myself that I have discovered the simple and complete way to make everyone's life better. After a few minutes of thought, and realizing that I had to get back on the road so I wasn't late, I figured out that what I discovered was not that groundbreaking after all. The five simple steps are relatively straightforward, and you probably know most of them, but like me you never give them much thought as to how much they influence your life. So here they are, simple and easy: (1) Know your audience, (2) Show people respect, (3) Sell before you close, (4) Quit selling after you close the deal, and (5) Pick your battles.

In the following chapters I will talk in detail on each point listed above. I will share stories of sales scenarios that should work, no matter what you sell. I will also give you the example of how my wife could have sold me on the idea of cleaning the shower, solidifying how this also applies to married life. After all, we are all salespeople. It's just a matter of what we are selling at the time.

I suggest that if you are reading this book hoping to gain insight, you may want to apply each chapter to your own personal experience. If you are reading this for business, think of a customer or scenario you have witnessed and analyze it. If you are reading this for marriage advice, think of a scenario when this could have applied to you or your spouse. I have also come to realize that writing these ideas down makes them easier to remember and adapt. So, go find a pad of paper and a pen. Don't worry, I will wait for you.

In case you were wondering, I never talked to my wife about this after that night. I am not sure she even remembers we had the conversation. It has taken me a few years to write this book. When she reads the book for the first time, hopefully she will not be too upset that I shared this story. Also, hopefully she will understand how that night became the inspiration for this book. And I should also mention that she had two kidney stones at the time. I am not sure if it is relevant, but I guess I need to mention all the facts surrounding the story.

Chapter 2
Know your Audience (And do your homework)

Every one of us is born a salesperson. From the time you were able to point and talk, you were selling. Some of us developed this skill better than others, but we all sell. Let me give you an example. When you were a baby, you cried to get fed or changed. As you got older, and learned to talk, you learned there were better ways to get food. You may have pointed at the shelf and said cookie. Or you went over to the closed toy box and said ball. Both of these had the same results, you got what you wanted. Some of you might have said "I love you Mommy," to avoid being punished for breaking her favorite vase while playing tackle football in the living room. I never would have done anything like that.

As you get older, you develop your skills. Have you ever talked a friend into eating a bug, breaking a window, cutting a class, or some other act of maleficence? How did you do it? Did you call them a chicken? Or maybe you told them they would become popular after they performed this minor infraction. Either way, you exploited their need for acceptance so you could be entertained at their expense, especially if they got caught. As a young person, I was the one who antagonized everyone to do the wrong thing. The nice thing about being in that position is that you usually don't get in trouble. Now that I think of it, not much has changed in my adult life.

By the same token, selling is nothing more than trying to fulfill a basic emotional need of the buyer, only without the entertainment factor. As a child when you tell a parent you love them, they feel warm inside, and you get your cookie. When you talked your friend into breaking the window, you were playing on their need to be accepted. Selling is nothing more than that. Think about it, we buy things to fill a basic emotion, whatever it may be. A perfect example is the automobile you drive. You may have purchased it for its great fuel economy, or because it has extra room for traveling, and your whole family fits in it. Or maybe you bought it because you like the color. If we bought cars for the purpose they were intended for, a conveyance, we would all drive the same model and color. Car makers know their audience and that emotions play into any buying decision. So that is why so many models, colors, and options are offered.

So how does this apply to the title of this chapter? Think about the examples mentioned above. If your friend whom you are trying to convince to break a window had been told by his parents that one more incident will result in him being shipped off to military school, you may have a harder time convincing him to break the window. His need to stay out of military school trumps the emotion of being popular.

Think about the last sales call you made. What did you know about your customer? One of the biggest mistakes I see are salespeople who are more concerned about selling their product than about how it fills the customer's needs. You can be selling the best product in the industry, but if it doesn't fill a need, your customer will probably not buy it. The best way to figure out the need is to know your audience.

In the case of my wife and me, she knew how I felt about starting conversations before I go to bed. She knew her audience, yet failed to accept the keys I have given her. She did not use the information she had, and just went right to selling me on the idea. Had she proposed cleaning her parents shower idea earlier in the evening, it may have been met with less or no resistance. If you know me well, you would know there are three times not to approach me with a question or opportunity. They are when I first arrive home from work, when I am watching television, and when I am going to bed. When I get home from work, I want a few minutes to unwind from the stress of work and traveling. If I am watching television, especially sports, my focus is on the game, not on what you are telling me. Chances are I may agree to whatever you ask, but it is only because I was not paying attention and will never remember it. And I think I have made it pretty clear how I feel about conversations at bed time.

She chose to ignore the keys, and proceeded with her agenda. She was going to sell me on the idea of cleaning the shower. She was trying to feed on my emotions of pleasing her and making her parents happy. These are very strong emotional selling techniques, but they usually will not work when my stronger need for sleeping was dominant. Had this same conversation taken place earlier that night (assuming I was not watching sports), the answer might have been a simple "yes." But then I would have never written this book.

Knowing your audience applies to all marriages and relationships. I have seen many friends date, move in together and even get married, only to split up soon thereafter. The biggest culprit in why they split is because they never talk. Not to say that they live in a silent home, but rather they have no idea of what motivates their partner. They get engrossed in the newness of their "love," and they forget to understand what makes their partner tick or how to better understand them. Again, don't get me wrong, I am not advocating that love is not a good reason to get together. I feel that it should be only one of the many reasons. Communication is important to have in both sales and relationships. If you begin a relationship not knowing about your partner, you are bound to fail.

This not only works with conversations, but on any issue. The worst time to talk about a vacation is right after you spent a lot of money on a major repair for the house or car. If your spouse had a difficult week at work, it's not a good idea to schedule a hectic weekend of activities without checking first. It is also not a good idea to suggest an all steak restaurant if your spouse does not eat red meat. These are just a few examples of understanding your spouse that will help solidify a relationship. Knowing more about your spouse will improve your relationship.

The best example of this is golf. I love golf. I would play every day if I could. My wife knows this and is very comfortable with it. She allows me (yes, I said allows.) to play as much as I can, as long as it does not interfere with family or other commitments. She is good about me playing on holidays because I get home early, and we have the afternoon to visit with family. However, I know enough to not play if we have plans and it might make us late. It works for us. One reason is that we talk through these things. If I am going to play twice in a weekend, I always make sure we have no plans that will be compromised (it doesn't hurt to throw in a date night as well).

The same holds true in business. No matter how good your product is, if you call on the wrong day, you will never have success. I have made it a point to try to avoid calling on clients the last day of the month. They are busy trying to close out month-end business and are very distracted. I have also asked customers which day they cut checks and try not to call on that day. What business owner wants to hear about how he can spend more money the day he just signed away thousands of dollars.

Now let's look at why customers buy. I like to use copy machine sales as a great example. I never sold them, but almost every business needs one and it is a mid to high capital expenditure. Usually a business will not think about buying a copy machine until the current machine breaks, so selling one is tough enough. But assume you have the most technologically advanced copy machine in the industry. It copies at record speed, collates, staples, faxes, replaces all your pc printers, makes coffee, and convinces your wife that going out for beers after work is necessary. That would be a machine that would sell itself and everyone would want one.

Unfortunately, that machine does not exist; at least not at the time of this writing. But even the best machine that sells itself will not sell to the customer who just took delivery of a new machine the day before. The first rule of sales is to identify whether or not there is a need. There are many ways to get this information, but the best is to ask a lot of questions. Whether it's in sales or marriage, the biggest mistake is to assume or skip the question stage and move right to selling. I have seen many salesmen walk into a customer's office and begin selling the product before they ever learned if there is a need. All they did was waste the customer's and their valuable time and energy. If you think about it, this is a very basic first step. If a car salesman appeared at your front door one day and began telling you why his model car is great and you need to buy it, how would you react? If you just bought a car, you may be asking where he was last week when you made your purchase. If you just lost your job, you may cut him short and tell him you are not in a position to buy right now. Or you may just shut the door on him because he is bothering you at home. Either way, he just wasted a call on a non-qualified buyer. That may be one of the reasons car salesmen don't go door to door.

Getting to know your customer is the first key in knowing your audience. Spending time to get to know them personally and professionally will save you time now and in the future. When I go to see a customer for the first time, I always tell them I am not here to sell you something on this visit, although I really am. On the first visit, I am there to learn a little more about the customer and his business so when the time is right, I can offer him the best solution to his problems. I also ask for a tour of the facility. Some companies spend millions of dollars on their buildings and machinery and love to show it off.

The next step is to remember to take notes. You may not have to write them all down, but it does help. I like to listen more and write my notes after I leave. It works for me, but everyone is different. Notes are not just about what your potential prospect says, or what keys you see to selling him your product, but also, it's about what objects you see around you. If you see something in the office, make a comment about it, it may get him talking and help to let his guard down. This will allow you to probe deeper to find out information about what you really came for. If he has a bunch of NASCAR memorabilia, ask him who is favorite driver is or if he saw the race last weekend. I once visited a client in North Carolina who had a degree from both The University of North Carolina and Duke University. These two schools are bitter basketball rivals. I had to ask how it came to be that someone could attend both schools, and of course where his allegiance might lie. It got him talking and before we knew it, he was telling me everything

I would ever want to know about his buying cycles and what he did not like about our competitors he was currently using.

I must warn you though to be genuine when asking questions. This lends more credence to knowing your audience. Don't act like you know about a subject if you really don't. In the previous paragraph, I mentioned NASCAR. It is OK to mention the memorabilia, but do not fake your knowledge about the subject. A true fan can spot a bullshitter in a heartbeat. I use NASCAR as my example because I spend a lot of time in the south, and most southerners love racing (I realize there is more to the south than racing, but in my business, this stereotype is pretty accurate). I have never been to a NASCAR event, but I know who most of the drivers are and watch the races on TV every week when I can. If I miss it, I make sure to check the newspaper or ESPN and see who won and what happened with the big-name drivers. When Becky sees me watching a race, she says I am "doing my homework." I do it so I can talk about the subject and it gets the customer involved in a conversation.

Whether it is racing, sports, antiques, horses, collectibles, or any other hobby, it's OK to show an interest, just don't try to fake how much you know.
Sometimes it is better to admit you know nothing, and just notice something that looks interesting. I once noticed a very odd chair in a customer's office. I asked him how old it was and if it had some significant meaning. He went on to tell me the story of the king who owned this chair and how he came to acquire it. That conversation stemmed into others and before long we were talking about business. He is a customer now and often tells me one of the things that got me in the door was how I noticed his prize chair.

There is an age-old adage that people buy from people and do business with friends. Think about how much easier it would be to sell to someone if you knew more about that person. Once you get to know a prospect, you can start to ask questions about their buying cycles, their needs for your product, and maybe the weaknesses of your competitors. By the same token, if you know when and how to approach your spouse or significant other with questions or desires, you both may get better results and live a little happier.

Chapter 3
Show People Respect

When I pulled over and starting writing my notes for this book idea, I wondered if this is really a necessary chapter for a book on selling and relationships. It is common knowledge to always show respect to others. Hopefully, it was one of the first things your parents taught you as a child. Yet I have seen a total lack of respect from some salespeople that I have traveled with from time to time. They don't mean to be disrespectful, they are just more focused on convincing a prospect that they need to buy the product.

Respect is a simple action that everyone desires. I have heard many people say that respect needs to be earned, but I think that saying is more relevant to the respect others show you. Respect should be given to everyone, no matter who they are or what their position in life might be. When you meet someone new, the biggest way to turn them off is to disrespect them. After you get to know them, you may form opinions of those people, but it should not affect showing the respect they deserve. It is one of the most courteous things you can do, and it doesn't cost you a thing. It can be as simple as how you greet a new prospect to knowing not to talk to your spouse when they are reading a book or watching the Browns play (yes, I am a Cleveland fan, and someday they will win it all).

My first example of respect goes back again to my wife and what prompted this book. She did not show respect for my need to sleep that night, knowing I needed to get up early the next morning. Don't get me wrong, I am not saying that she is disrespectful (I want to stay married after all), she just thought of her agenda first before considering mine. She may say that I was not respectful of her wishes, or I would have said yes to her request right away. But she was selling me on the idea, so she was wrong and I was right. Had she approached me earlier in the night, we could have had this same conversation, and she would have gotten what she wanted and we both could have been OK with the results. But instead, I am writing this book.

Think about some of the couples you know. I bet you can list numerous examples of how people do not show respect to each other. It could be something as simple as not calling home when you are going to be late, or inviting people your spouse does not like to a party. The bottom line is that showing respect is a very simple thing to do, but is one of the easiest ones to overlook.

Respect is not just about what to say and do, but also about what not to say or do. We had some friends who were throwing a dinner party for about 15 people. In the middle of dinner, our host began talking about their spouse, going into some rather explicit details of things that really should not be spoken about at dinner parties. While this may be an acceptable conversation for people of like thoughts and actions, it wasn't for the group that was in attendance that evening. The spouse was mortified and ran out of the room red-faced. This ended our night out. This was a blatant lack of respect.

In business, I have seen many instances of complete lack of respect. It has ranged from not allowing the prospect to participate in the conversation, to arguing with him about the information he provides. There are many ways to disrespect a client. One way is not showing any appreciation for the person's position in the company. Imagine that you are that copier salesperson I like to use as my example, and you are calling on a client. You begin the call talking with the office manager, who cannot approve the sale, but definitely can say no to the sale. You ignore their status in the sales cycle as an influencer and try to climb over top of them to get to the final decision maker; the person who can write the check. Again, you may have the best product out there, but when the boss comes and asks for input from the office manager, he/she will remember how you treated them and more often than not, your competitor will get the sale. I am not advocating that you should not try to get to the decision maker, just do not forget to spend time with the influencers and respect their input and time. They can be your best allies or your biggest enemies.

The next biggest lack of respect that I see is undermining your client's (or spouse's) intelligence. This is usually unintentional, but I have seen the mistake hundreds of times. In business, you want to upsell your product against your competitor, but that is a very fine line. If you are selling your copy machine, you want to stress your selling points, but not at the expense of what the customer is currently using. If you compare the features against your competitor, make sure you upsell your product or service and not down sell your competitor. If you begin in attack mode, and that client has purchased from that competitor in the past, he may feel that you are attacking his intelligence. Making references to a competitor's product as being inferior can be construed as telling the customer he is not very intelligent. After all, an intelligent person would never buy an inferior product.

The same can be said in marriage. Pointing out an error that your spouse made may seem like you are trying to help fix a problem, but more often, it is perceived as a dig on their intelligence. Not that this has ever happened in my life, but imagine if your spouse stopped at the gas station one day to fill up the car. However, she pulled up to the full-service lane. (For those of you who do not know what that is, it is where attendants from the station come out to pump your gas and wash your windows. They also charge about fifty cents more per gallon). The message that you want to relay is that your spouse unnecessarily spent ten dollars, but there are two ways it can be perceived. If you say something like, "I can't believe you went to the full-service lane, do you know how much that cost?" You will get your point across but the end result may not be too favorable. While you may not realize it, your response may be heard like this: "I cannot believe that you are so dumb to pay all that extra money when you could have gotten out of the car and done it yourself." Your spouse would be insulted and feel that their intelligence has been challenged. The better way to approach this might go something like this: "Thank you for stopping by and filling up the car. Next time we get gas, I will show you how to pump it yourself and it will save us $10 and then we can go to the movies with the money we save. You will have gotten your point across and shown the benefits of the better decision. In addition, you will have shown your spouse that you appreciate her gesture, even if it was a costly one. Remember, and this probably applies more to men than women; if you make a statement, and it can be perceived in two ways, your spouse is likely to assume you meant it in the more negative way.

Finally, and I cannot stress this enough; respect the time of the person with whom you are speaking. Try to schedule appointments whenever possible. If a client agrees to meet with you, but tells you up front that they don't have much time, keep your message to the point and get out of there. If your client says he has 5 minutes, wrap it up in four, thank him for giving you that time, and see if you can schedule a follow up. I did this exact thing one time; I wrapped up an abbreviated sales call in 4 minutes and told the client I appreciated the time he gave me. I asked for another appointment later, but he said he could shuffle a few things around and if I had the time, he would like to hear more. I ended up staying about 2 hours, left with all the information I needed to build a competitive quote against my competitor, and had the customer convinced that my product was the best fit for what he needed to conduct business. On my next call, I won the account and he is still a customer today.

If you show that kind of respect, you will get another appointment, and maybe you will get the sale. The same holds true in marriage. As I stated earlier, if Becky would have approached me earlier in the day, not when I was ready for bed, the results would have been a lot different. Don't interrupt your spouse when they are watching their favorite shows. Don't pull them away from a phone call with friends. The respect you show will take you far.

I have one last point on the topic of respect. This applies to both business and relationships; cell phone etiquette. If you are visiting a customer, turn off, mute, or leave your cell phone in the car. Never answer a call or return an email or text when meeting with a client. I had this happen to me when traveling with a salesperson once. His phone rang and he got up and walked out of the customer's office to take the call. When he was finished, he walked back in and sat down, not saying a word about the call. Even though this was an established customer, I could tell he was a little put off by this. As it turned out, the salesman's granddaughter was in the hospital and it was his wife calling to give him an update. While that is an exception to the general rule, a simple apology and a quick explanation upon return would have made the client feel a lot better.

The same holds true in relationships. What message do you think you are sending if you interrupt a conversation with your spouse to take a phone call? You are in essence telling your spouse that what they have to say is not as important as the call. Or what I feel is even worse is picking up your phone and emailing or texting while in the middle of a conversation. This, in my opinion, is one of the most disrespectful things you can do. The message you are sending to your spouse is that whatever I have to do on my phone is more important than anything you need to be telling me. There will be situations when this cannot be avoided, but as a general rule, when your spouse is talking, give them your undivided attention, especially if they were courteous enough to wait till the commercial to begin to talk to you. If you need to use your phone immediately, show your spouse some courtesy. Say something like, "I am sorry to interrupt, I know what you are saying is important, and we can discuss it further, but I just forgot I needed to send out this email immediately. As soon as I finish, we can continue our discussion." Your spouse should appreciate your acknowledgement that her thoughts are important, or she may throw something at you. In case the latter happens, make sure she is closer to the pillows than she is to the dishes.

Chapter 3.5
Don't Lie

I really think this subject is important, but I also think it is straightforward and obvious, that it doesn't require a whole chapter.

Let me clarify one thing right away. This half chapter was an afterthought. The reason I started writing this book was because of something that happened between Becky and me. However, she never lied to me on this or any other subject, at least as far as I know.

I was writing the chapter on respect, and I started thinking about how people use deceit and trickery to sell. I thought it was important enough to discuss.

I have seen many professional salespeople lie to sell their product. I like to think it's unintentional, but I know better. Lying may gain you the first sale, but it will never get you a long-term customer. Lies will always come out, and the longer they build, the harder they are to overcome. It is difficult to tell a customer bad news. Sometimes your product may not be the best fit for your customer's needs. Sometimes your product may be experiencing problems that affect performance and results. Deception only leads to customer dissatisfaction.

I was selling a software product and the technology was a little dated. The product was solid, and it did fit the need of some, but not every customer. I could have sold it as a proven product and told every customer what they wanted to hear, but at the end of the day, all you really have are your principles. No one can take that away from you. I felt it was better to tell the truth about the product and let it fit for the right customer. If it did not fit the customer's needs, I did not want to sell it to him.

As for relationships, there is one hard and fast rule; do not lie. The only exception to that rule is if you are throwing a surprise party for your spouse or you ate your spouse's cupcake. In the case of the cupcake, always blame the dog; however, it does help to have a dog. All humor aside, lying in a relationship is a deal killer. If you are lying, stop it and come clean. And guys (I can only relate to you since I am one), if you think you are getting away with a lie, you're not. They know. You are not that good.

That's all I have to say about that subject.

Chapter 4
Sell Before You Close

This too may seem pretty straight forward, but you would be surprised how many times I have seen it happen. The group of sales people I see that are most guilty of this are car sales people. More often than not, when you shop for a car, you take one for a test drive. When you come back, the first words out of the salesperson are "What can we do to put you in this car today?" To their defense, they know that the odds of you coming back after you leave are low, so the pressure sale is a predominant tactic. But who among us loves to go car shopping, except for me. I understand the art of the high-pressure sale, and I will use their sales tactics against them, sometimes just for my amusement. It may be why some car salespeople hide when they see me entering the dealership.

In the case of Becky and the shower, she was ready to close me before selling me on the idea. She assumed that my desire to make her and her parents happy would trump any other emotion. I can only assume that she didn't think she needed to sell me on the idea. Normally she would be right, but not that night. Had she started by telling me that she noticed the shower was getting stained, and that her parents cannot seem to clean it as well as they used to, and then led into how much they would appreciate it, I am sure it would have been a much easier sell. However, she wanted to close the deal quickly. Maybe she was trying to respect my time by getting it out quickly so I could get some sleep. Whatever the motive, it did not work.

Whatever you are trying to sell, whether it's a car, copier, or convincing your spouse to spend time with your annoying friend that they cannot stand, you have to sell them on the idea first before you close. I have seen many young sales people walk into a client's office ready to close a deal without ever asking the correct questions to see if the product meets the needs of the customer. If you are shopping for a car, what are the important things you are looking for? It could be safety, room for your family, ability to tow the camper, fuel mileage, or a myriad of other things. But if you head to your local car dealer and he says, "I have a great deal on a Yugo, what do we have to do to get you in this car today?" How likely are you to buy it, let alone do any business at that location. The salesperson did not take the time to get to know you and your needs. They did not find the right fit for you; instead tried to force you into what they wanted to sell that day.

It is also important to understand the difference between trying to close the deal and using trial closes. A trial close might be something as simple as getting the customer or your spouse to begin to agree with benefits of the features you are selling. An example of this would be a copier salesmen, who might ask if a new copier that saves 30% annually on toner costs is something that would be important to him in his decision. I have heard many sales professionals talk about FAB's, which stand for Features, Advantages and Benefits. Features are easy; they are the product offerings that make your product special. The advantages are what makes the product work better for the customer. However, the benefits are the hardest and are always the ones that seemed to get overlooked. These benefits are also what can be used as trial closes. A long-time mentor of mine mentioned that if you cannot apply some kind of feel-good benefit, you cannot use it to close. That feel-good benefit may be financial, image, or something else, but the customer has to see the benefit. In the case of the copier salesperson, the 30% savings on toner is a cost that he won't be paying if he buys the new copier.

Trial closes in a relationship are just as important. Becky tried a trial close on me with the shower scenario. She played upon my desire to make her parents happy and to be helpful to her. But in her case, she moved right into the close and skipped the previous steps, hence my reluctance to say yes right off the bat.

I once made a call on a customer with another salesperson. He did his homework, found out what the customer was using currently, and had a list of selling points as to why the product he was selling was better. He went in ready to sell and close on his product. The only problem was that the customer's business model changed, and the current product was going to be phased out. He tried to close his product and I could see the customer was not interested, so I asked a simple question, "How is your current product working for you?" He was very forthcoming in telling us that certain laws and regulations had forced him to change his business practices and the current product would be useless to him in 6 months. After knowing that, we changed our sales strategy to sell him on one of our products that would meet his future needs. We were also able to offer him a way to dispose of his current product, so he would not have to worry about that.

We sold him on the idea that we could solve all his problems. We closed the deal, and believe it or not, price was never really an issue.

Using trial closes also work in relationships, as long as the statements push towards positive reinforcement. Which statement is more likely to be met with a better response: (1) Honey, we are going out with Larry (the guy you despise) tonight, or (2) Honey, I know you don't really like Larry, but he was able to get tickets to the sold-out show you wanted to see, and he asked us to go with him. Both statements have the same end result; you are going to be spending time with a person whom you are not especially fond of. However, in the second scenario, the thought of going to a sold-out show might weigh more than spending time with someone like Larry. It is all about selling the idea before you try to close it.

Getting to the close is the easiest part of the sales process. It's where you get to ask for the order or in the case of marriage, you get to ask for what you want. The hard part about closing is that if you close before you sell, your rate of success will be significantly lower. Measuring the success is as simple as more sales, or getting a positive response from your spouse. In the case of Becky, selling before closing would have increased her success rate, but then I would have never written this book.

You may be saying to yourself about now that all these ideas are pretty straight forward, and why am I reading this. I know this stuff, I am better than this. The truth is that you may be. I think I am. But I have found myself skipping some of these steps because I did not prepare or did not plan. The end results are nearly always the same and very predictable. If you don't follow the steps, you are not going to get the sale, or you are not going to have a happy spouse.

Chapter 4.5
Be Ready to Handle Objections

In my original version, this half chapter also did not exist. Truthfully, had I been a little more diligent on getting this book published, it probably never would have made it. But I guess that is why they call it a work in process.

When Becky was trying to sell me on cleaning the shower, she was ready to handle the objections. She might not have been prepared for them, but she did have answers for them. My guess is that she just expected me to say yes. But she was ready to overcome my objections with reasons why it was a good idea.

Practicing handling objections is just as important as the selling and closing. Try to imagine what reasons your customer may say no, so you can try to overcome them. If you need help, just listen to the next telemarketer who calls you. These people are well trained. Have you ever been able to say no to them just once and they leave you alone? I had a person call me for a donation on the phone recently. I was on the way out the door and didn't have time to listen, and quite frankly wasn't really interested in donating to his cause, so I told him what I thought was the quickest way to get rid of him. I told him that I just lost my job and money was going to be tight for a while. To his credit, he came back asking for a smaller donation or maybe a deferred donation that I could start a few months later when I got back on my feet. I thought I was pretty smart using that excuse, but he was ready for it.

In business, the number one objection has to be price. The company I worked for sells a premium priced product, and are always higher than the competitor. It is not uncommon to hear that the price is too high. But even when you have the lowest price, some people will want to negotiate just to see if they can do better.

When I am confronted about price, I never lower it in front of the customer. It sends the wrong message. It tells them that you did not come in with your best price. That is why the car salesman has to "ask his boss" if he can do any better. He wants you to think that he gave you the best deal he could and only someone higher can approve a better deal. I look at price objection as a buying queue. I think to myself, this customer is asking me to tell him why he should pay more for my product versus my competitor.

The first thing I ask is "compared to what?" You need to know what his baseline is for pricing. It is usually your competitor, but sometimes it could be you. Maybe your price has gone up considerably since the last purchase. This is why you need to practice overcoming objections.

I was calling on a customer and the price objection came up. His comparison was my competitor. I asked for the specifications so we could do a side by side comparison. I told him to cover up the competitor's pricing, as I was not concerned about it. I just wanted to make sure we were both quoting the same options. After the comparison, we found out that our product had many more options than the competitor. My question back to the customer was, should we strip our product down or would you like to make the competitor come up to our specs. This only works if you can show a benefit for having the additional content. In this particular case, the customer liked the additional options we offered, and was willing to pay for them. We got the sale and didn't have to lower our price.

But what objections do you face in relationships? Whether you are booking a vacation, buying a new set of golf clubs, or trying to get your spouse to clean the shower, there may always be an objection. By understanding them and preparing for them, you may overcome them.

All I can say is that it is important to sell the benefits of the decision, and make sure that you prepare for the objections.

Chapter 5
Quit Selling After You Close the Deal

I was hesitant about this chapter because like all the others, it seems pretty straight forward. It is, but I see this mistake way too often. I don't want to categorize one person or one group of people, but I think spouses (and Becky in particular) are the guiltiest of this mistake. Once you close the sale, why do you want to keep selling? What is the benefit?

Let's go back to our copier salesman example again. He has done everything correct; he knew his audience and the players in the decision process. He knew the decision makers and the influencers. He knew the client was in need of the product. He showed proper respect to all of the people in the decision-making process. He sold the product on the merits that would benefit the customer. He was able to show financial and feel-good reasons to buy the product. He ran a few trial closes, got the customer to agree to the benefits, and received a signed order. Then it was time to shake hands, find out where to get the purchase order, talk about the delivery, and get out. But not our copier sales guy. For some reason he wanted to keep selling the product features.

I applaud this salesman because he has a strong passion for his product. But once you get the deal, it's time to leave. I am not saying that it's not important to make sure the client understands all the features of your product, but after the close is not the time. I would recommend in this scenario, that the salesman sets up another appointment once the product is delivered. This will allow him to go over all the other features that might be beneficial to the customer and the end users.

The product that I have been selling for nearly 25 years has many benefits, and I would love to be able to show each one of them to my customers. However, there is not enough time in a sales call, and quite frankly most customers don't have the time to hear them all. So, I choose the important ones, use them to close the deal, and then move on. Don't get me wrong, I make sure that the customer knows about every feature. However, I make follow up appointments to make sure the users and influencers are involved, since they may be the ones who are using the product and taking advantage of these options.

The previous example is what I would call a rookie mistake. Experienced salespeople usually know when to stop talking, but it's very easy to keep selling after the fact, even for the best of us.

You may wonder what are the issues of continuing to close after the sale is done. You run the risk of alienating the decision maker. He has given you the order and you keep selling him. He may feel that you do not value his time. He may become disinterested. He may think your product is too complicated and has too many options that he will not need. He may consider shopping for a lower option product. I think the biggest thing is that you risk the decision-maker changing his mind. That means you may lose the sale, and nobody wants that.

Professional salespeople usually learn from this mistake and change in a short process. Hopefully they learn from a mentor, and not because they lost a sale. Your spouse (or you, if you are guilty of this) may not learn as fast because there is less to lose. Becky likes to keep selling after the close. I know she is not doing it consciously; she just wants to make sure that I understand the benefits of doing what she asks.

In relating this to relationships, let's assume your spouse asks you to do something around the house, like wash the car. Your spouse may sell you on the fact that you are going someplace special and it would be nice to arrive in a clean car. She may offer to make you a special dinner or let you (yes, I said let you) play golf this weekend. Once you agree, it's time to say thank you and move on to the next subject. It's OK to talk about details, like making sure the interior is swept, or the windows get cleaned, but don't keep selling on getting the car washed. Trying to sell after the close in a relationship will ultimately get the response of "I already said I would do it."

This leads perfectly into my next point. Sometimes, no matter how hard you try, you may not win the sale. Whether it is to a customer or to your spouse, sometimes the answer is going to be no. When this happens, it is always best to say thank you for the time, and then regroup. I am not advocating giving up without trying, but there is a fine line between trying and being pushy. It is very hard to manage this skill, both in sales and relationships. I will go into more detail about this in the next chapter, but keep that in mind.

In the case of the shower, Becky glossed over some of the early steps, tried to close me, and when I said no, she kept trying to sell me. This is an example of where the answer was going to be no. I wish I had a 100% positive close rate, but nobody does. She asked, I said no, but then she kept trying to sell me on how it would make her happy, and how appreciative her parents would be. I give her credit, she never gives up, but sometimes it is better to stop selling and maybe try again later.

The bottom line is respect. Respect the time of your customer or you spouse. Respect the decision that is made. Respect the job you did selling the product or idea, and finally, respect yourself. Selling after the close shows a lack of respect.

Chapter 6
Pick Your Battles

I thought about this chapter a lot. The premise of me writing this book is that Becky did not know the correct sales techniques to close me on cleaning her parents shower. Some may say that bringing this proposal to me at night, before I was going to bed, was not picking her battles correctly. However, that is not where I was planning to go with this chapter.

When I refer to picking your battles, I am talking about knowing when to stop. As you recall, when Becky asked me at night, I said no. The barrage of why's just made the matter worse. Picking your battles just means using all the tools I have talked about in the previous chapters and knowing when to give up. Had Becky accepted my no response as a final answer, she could have broached the subject the next day when I was rested, and she could have sold and closed me on the idea. I would have probably said yes at that time. I know I really don't have a choice in these matters, but it sure is nice to think I do.

Let's see how this might apply in business. Picking your battles may be something as simple knowing who you can and cannot sell. Our friend the copier salesmen, for example, would have a hard time selling a copier to a customer whose niece sells a competitor's product, especially if that is his spouse's only niece. Picking your battles is more about knowing which customers you can sell and the ones you cannot. It is about using your time effectively and efficiently.

I am not suggesting that you do not call on this customer, because things may change and it is important to build a relationship. His niece might have gotten a new job and is out of the equation. Everything is fluid, so it is important to stay in touch with any potential client. Any experienced salesperson will tell you that you cannot sell to everyone. It may be product preference, it may be a previous relationship with a competitor, or it may be that your product is not the best fit for the customer's needs. Whatever the case, things do change and staying in touch may lead to something in the future. A timely courtesy call to a customer like this may not result in an immediate sale, but it could lead to something down the road. Picking your battles may also mean knowing how much time to spend with a client based on his potential.

How does it apply to your relationships though? Picking your battles refers to understanding what is important to your spouse, knowing how and when to ask, and knowing when to walk away. It probably would not be a good idea to schedule a Sunday family visit at the same time one of the biggest football games of the season is on TV. Or would it be prudent to ask about taking a golf weekend when the house needs painted and you agreed to do it? Again, that is probably not the best time to bring up the subject.

There is a right and wrong time for everything. The key to a good sale or a great relationship is to know the difference, and capitalize on it at the right time. If you have an appointment with a client who is ready to be closed, and you find out that he just had a traumatic event happen in his personal life, it might be smart to reschedule. Most probably the attention needed by the customer will not be there, and you may not get the right response for which you were looking.

Picking your battles also goes hand in hand with developing a relationship with a customer. By not taking advantage of a negative situation, you solidify your long-term relationship with the customer.

Taking advantage of a situation may land you a sale, but it probably will not get you a customer for life. I had a situation like this. I had an appointment with a customer who was just about ready to give me the sale. I had done all the right things in the sales process.

We just had a few minor points to cover, but I was confident that I would close the deal on this call. When I arrived at the customer's location, he met me and we went to his office. Because I got to know the customer, I could tell that his mind was not on the business at hand. I asked him if he was OK. He told me that his grandson was just taken to the hospital for surgery. I asked him if it was serious, and he said he wasn't sure. I then asked him why he wasn't there, since I could tell it was looming on him. He said he didn't want to miss our appointment, since he knew I travelled so far to see him. I told him that family was more important than anything I had to say that day, and I insisted that he leave right away to go see his grandson. I could have used this opportunity to rush him through the close and maybe get him to sign a deal. Or I could have lost the sale because I did not respect his time and feelings. I did not insist that he leave our appointment as part of a sales technique, it was just the right and decent thing to do. Family always comes first. But I can tell you that his grandson is great now. I went back a few weeks later, and we closed the sale. He still to this day talks about how I passed on an easy sale because I cared more about him than my sale. The sale was a win, but the respect I gained made me feel even better.

Let's pick on our friend the car salesman again for another example. You walk in to buy a car, and the salesman talks you into a car with a payment higher than your budget may allow. He may get the sale, because he sold you on some benefits of the higher priced car. However, every month when you make the payment, you will probably remember feeling that you were pressured into that higher priced car. If you feel taken, what are the chances you will ever return and do business with him again? My guess is never.

The bottom line is that it is better to look at the person than the sale. Relationships build better customers and knowing when to strike and when to walk away will make that bond stronger.

Chapter 7
The Close (Final Chapter)

Selling is easy. The close is the hard part. Think about that for a moment. If you are passionate about what you are selling, it is easy to sell. It may be a product for your company, or selling your wife on the reason why it's a good idea to play golf this weekend. It's the close that is the difficult part of the equation. It could be difficult convincing your wife that playing golf is a good idea. Fortunately for me, my wife is very understanding and encouraging about my golf passion. I am lucky in that respect.

Closing a book is just as hard. Conventional wisdom says make your points and close by reiterating your ideas in a summary format. It is what every good business school will teach you, whether you are making a sales call or preparing a presentation. I don't think it's that easy with a book. If I were to just rehash the last 6 chapters, you might not read this one. Even worse, you might just read this chapter and get the summary of my ideas. You would then miss all of my wit and insight.

I have decided to go a little off script and end the book my way. I will mix a little of the common practice in with a few more stories, and hopefully you will have a few more laughs as you read on.

As I mentioned earlier, I have been selling for about 25 years and married even longer. It really doesn't make me an expert on either subject. It has however given me some insight on what works and what does not. I like to think that I have a good understanding of what it takes to be successful in sales, but I have made a few blunders along the way. I hope that I have learned from them and hopefully you will too.

The same goes with relationships. Like most, I have made my share of mistakes, but hopefully they have made me a better husband and person. The key is to learn and not repeat the mistakes in the future. It could be something as simple as remembering that your spouse likes pink roses better than red roses. It may be making sure you call home if you are going to be late. FYI, not calling when you are going to be late and then bringing home the wrong color flowers is a double whammy. You may think that one is making up for the other, but remember you need to do your homework and know your audience. Not that I would have any personal experience on this. I always call home when I will be late.

On the flowers subject, or any gift for that matter, it doesn't have to be a makeup for doing something wrong. Sometimes it is nice to get something for no particular reason. I was riding with a salesman who once stopped to get coffee and donuts for a customer before visiting. I thought it was a nice gesture till I found the only reason he was doing it was because he felt guilty about an issue that was not handled properly. A gift should not only be used as an apology, sometimes it can just be a thoughtful gesture.

I have a dealer who regularly goes to his customers' places of business and cooks lunch for their employees. He does it because he appreciates his customers, and it's a nice thing to do. I think he enjoys it as well. He doesn't expect anything in return, but it does pay off. His customers are loyal to him and his business.

I enjoy selling, but I also enjoy being sold. I understand the process and have a great deal of respect for those who truly understand and work through the steps.

You may have noticed that I picked on car salespeople a little in this book. I love to go car shopping. I like the art of negotiation, and I am not easily swayed by high pressure sales. Many of my friends take me when they go car shopping. The main reason is that I do my homework as a consumer. I try to know as much about the car and the deal as the salesperson. I have caught a few salespeople trying to alter the terms of our agreement. I had one try to extend my payment terms from 48 months to 60 months, thinking I would not realize it. He was wrong. I tell you this story because it is important to know that your customer has done their homework too. Today's consumer is more educated, and trying little "tricks" do more harm than good in the process.

In case you were wondering, I did buy the car, but left with an even better deal than what I originally agreed upon. The owner overheard the rather loud discussion, and came over to see what was going on. When he thought I was going to walk out and cancel the deal, he offered a better rate, lower price and threw in a few oil changes. He realized how valuable a satisfied customer is, and how devastating a disgruntled customer could be. He wanted to make sure that I left satisfied and felt like I was treated properly. He must have asked me three or four times, and even asked if there was anything else he could do for me.

Like I mentioned early in the book, we are all salespeople, just in varying degrees. We use the techniques to get the results we want, both in business and in personal life. Those of us who make sure we understand the process are usually more successful.

The bottom line is to remember that everything discussed in the previous chapters are common sense practices. Knowing your audience, showing respect, telling the truth, sell before you close a deal, quit selling after you close, and picking your battles; these are things we all do with little thought most of the time. But sometimes we forget one or two steps. I think I have dragged enough about how when Becky skipped a few of those steps, the results were less than what she anticipated.

So, remember these steps, write them down, rehearse your script for each, and maybe your success will increase. Whether you are looking for more sales, or just trying to get a few more rounds of golf approved by the boss each month, hopefully your close rate will be better.

I am going to close this book now. I will wait to see how the book is accepted by Becky. I may have to write a sequel of what happens after you write a book about something your wife did without her knowing about it. Keep your eyes open for that. In the meantime, good luck and I hope I helped. If not, I hope I made you laugh just a little.

Epilogue

I was going to skip this, but if I wrote an epilogue, I figured I could actually finish the book and quit adding half-chapters. After all, I was trying to keep this book at a minimum number of pages. Also, Becky said that I should write this and let you know what happened when she read the book for the first time. To start with, she did not remember the whole shower story, but after reading this book she did apologize for keeping me up that night. I did hear her laugh out loud a few times while she was reading the book. That was a pretty good sign, at least I thought so.

I did have to make a few revisions, but overall, she was very happy with the book and seemed to enjoy it. For those who are wondering, yes, we are still happily married, going very strong, and her kidney stones have passed. When I printed the book for her to edit, I think she wrote about as much as I typed on 8770 pages, but thankfully most of it was her take on the stories, and some quick- witted one-liners. If not, this book may have been twice as long and I may have lost interest in writing it.

I had a lot of fun writing and revising this book. It was a little difficult to envision writing, editing, and getting a book published. This may stop some people from trying. But believe me, if you have a passion to tell a story to the world, I strongly encourage you to try. The worst thing that can happen is that you never publish it or sell it, but at least you tried.

Thank you for purchasing my book. I hope you enjoyed reading it as much as I did writing it. Who knew that someone could write a book with a premise that was conceived around cleaning a shower? It just goes to show you that guys will do anything to get out of household chores. Perhaps my next book should be about how to do common household chores poorly, so that you never have to do them again. I'm experienced at that too. I can't remember the last time I had to do the dishes or the laundry.

Can You Sell It?

If you liked the book, tell your friends. If you didn't like it, don't tell anyone. Besides, they probably wouldn't believe that you read a book on a guy saying no to cleaning a shower anyway.

Goodbye for now.

www.ingramcontent.com/pod-product-compliance
Lightning Source LLC
Chambersburg PA
CBHW071108240526
45469CB00006BD/2384